DAVID BEDNALL

EVOCATION OF WELLS CATHEDRAL

MUSIC DEPARTMENT

OXFORD

UNIVERSITY PRESS

for Elsa van der Zee
with much love and gratitude, and in tribute to her knowledge and love of Wells Cathedral, particularly the Jesse Window

Evocation of Wells Cathedral

'O Radix Jesse'

DAVID BEDNALL

**Vox humana,
Bourdon + trem.**

A little faster but with freedom

* Wherever possible the second line down should be played on a clarinet or cromorne. If preferred simply incorporate it into the top line.

Pushing forwards slightly

Sempre incalzando
+ Flutes 4'
52
+ Foundations 4'
56
+ Swell Reeds 8' (Box closed)
60
rit.
+ Foundations 16'
+ Swell Reeds 16', 4'
64

Clifton Village, 28 July 2016